AS LIFE TRANSCENDS

AGRAJA P NAIR

Contents

Preface

This collection is a humble attempt of a wandering mind, that wish to explore the raw emotions, musings of a human soul and transcendence of life. These verses strive to capture fleeting beauty of love, desire to be loved, unwavering zeal for life and the shattered recesses of minds. The following is the poet's first attempt at recording silent musings of her mind. The poems written at different points of time is a journey through emotions where the poet hope the reader to find pieces of oneself, a whisper from the depths one was unaware of.

Acknowledgements

First and foremost, I would like to thank my senior Reymon Lopez, whose belief and support led to the very idea of this collection. A special thanks to my dear friends, Pooja and Akshara, who took the time to read, reflect and provide feedbacks on these poems. Also, a special mention to my mother who helped me in designing the cover page.

Thanks to all my friends, family and mentors who have encouraged my poetic attempts. Lastly, I thank Almighty God for helping me compose and complete this collection.

1. Revelation was you

Revelation was you to me…
Discovering a whole new universe.
I repeat…
A whole universe,
Not a mere constellation,
Was you to me.
In this Eureka, did I lose mine?
A Big Bang it was, I remember;
Where lights flashed and rocks crumbled,
Threads of fate tangled.
A Big Bang connecting your boundless –
boundaries to mine.
Now in you dissolved am I,
Dissolved in aesthetic wonder,
And in you engrossed are my musings and thoughts.

2. She

She was a tale - a folklore,
Mystic yet a dreaded frame.
A witch to be burned,
In the pyre of her dreams.
She was a rag doll with dead eyes,
With lips sewed from end to end.
A fine art with muted thoughts,
Furrowing deep into her rusty brain.
She was a warrior within and out,
Where ardent flames burned unknown.
Unrelenting warrior was she, an unsung lore;
A dark silhouette in generations to behold.

3. Siren

A siren lost in the darkest depths
Was she; a serene soul.
Deceptive were her scales,
Her fangs and her red blood eyes.
So was her nails and her fins.
Yet her voice carried her soul;
Her dreams and desires.
Her song, her voice lured,
Many a ship off their course.
It carried in it the ether
Where did float her unseen beauty;
A mermaid within a siren was she.
A siren lost in the darkest depths
Was she; a serene soul.
In her sleepless nights she did sing,
In the pale moonlight,
To the love of her life.
In the moonlit rocks and glistening sea,
She did turn glittering gold.
No longer was she a scary crippling frame,
Of bones and scales, dull and pale.
Her hair did flow
Shining in the silver stream.

She did glow with youth and love.
A beauty to behold.
A siren lost in darkest depths
Was she; a serene soul
Not one familiar in fairy tales.
Not one familiar with dreams and hopes.
But with the familiar stench
Of a wretched horror tale,
One long forgotten in the woods.
A soul hidden in the cramped corners,
Hiding in the bosom of secrets;
Where she herself was a dark secret.
Was she a siren. A mystic dream.
A fable. A Horror scene.
A siren lost in the darkest depths
Was she; a serene soul.
She did crave with every piece of her.
Not blood, flesh nor lust.
But love... to be loved.
Her every single piece of flesh
And soul did ache and ache.
Not a myth was she,
Nor was love a myth to her.
She did long to be embraced
By sunrays and morning breeze;
To wander off from the deepest depths.
A siren lost in the darkest depths,

Was she; a serene soul.
A mermaid within a siren.
A beauty to behold.

• 5 •

4. To be a Muse

I want to be your muse.
Not a poet, but a muse;
The one to touch your heart,
To be strangled in your thoughts.
To be felt by your lips.
I want to be a muse,
Not to wield a pen.
To flow through your fingertips,
To bleed through the ink,
To take form in your words.
I want to be your muse,
To be immortal.
Even when your ear forgets my voice,
Even when your eyes forget my smile,
Even when your hand no longer embraces,
Even when my name doesn't light your eyes.
I want you to be my poet,
For your words to embrace me.
So, when years fade away,
When you and me no longer exist;
I will be yours and you mine.

5. A Haiku on Her

She was a lone art,
Dripping wet with blood and tears
Beheld by blind eyes.

6. Shades of Brown

In a world where outlooks were judged,
Where hearts were embraced by envy,
Where shapes and shades judged the soul,
Hooded and wrapped she walked.
A dichotomy within distortions,
Echoing incoherent incantations.
Sighs from slithering tongues –
"Oh! Only if she was a shade fairer".
Face washes and beauty creams
Heaped in corners of her room,
Where once thrived the heart
That knew the art of love.
She was a canvas of history,
Each shade of her a legacy.
She was of earth and nature,
A shade of re-incarnations.
She was the revered dark Goddess,
Kali*. She was time and what was not time.
She was Krishna* with copper eyes,
Proud with stardust in her vein.
Now they preyed on her sunken soul,
Buried by goblins who seek fair shades.
Fret and fumes of malice deafened her,

Who screamed and roared aloud —
"Art of Beauty is fair and slim".
All they saw was her stature and her skin tone,
But not the stories she told.
*Kali- Hindu Goddess
*Krishna- Draupadi in the epic Mahabharata

7. At the Coffee table

A soft jazz and a warm coffee
With blurred unknown faces around,
The table at the corner awaited me-
A lone nest with silent paintings.
Gazing at the empty chair,
Weaving imaginary conversations;
A sip of coffee meant a word.
Two lines read meant a conversation.
Scribbling in my note meant
A laughter with you,
holding hands.
At last, I left the table alone.
The cup empty,
With notebook covered in pencil strokes
And a letter for you.

8. You

In dark silent nights
A faint moonlight was you;
Cold yet a warm embrace,
Humming soft lyrics untold.
A silver lining through the window sill
Never once opened even by the wind.
Yet you came alone… a shadow to the soul,
Left in corners behind.
Those moments where you talked
Endlessly in soft whispers,
Where time is a sea
Where you echoed in waves.
Your sound was my favourite music.
Your smile, my favourite painting.
Your words, my favourite poetry.
Your presence, my favourite place to be.
I now fear as clock ticks,
Will we see again?
Will you remain near?
Will I even be a part of your memories?
Tomorrow I might fade away from you,
As you forget my name and smile.
Yet, you will be the beloved chapter

Of my book,
Where the corner of the page
Will always be folded.

• 12 •

9. Love is a riddle

For me,
Love is a riddle- unanswered.
A poem I wrote where,
Lines left unrhymed,
Words were invisible.
Yet a scent filled my pores,
Distant and unfamiliar.
Love was a feeling swelling in me,
A tide long suppressed.
Love was not recognized,
When it knocked on the doors.
Window sills were locked.
Eyes closed.
Love was a stranger,
I yearned to behold;
Yet ignored.
Love was a shadow,
Left behind in the darkest roads.

10. The Lost Poetry of Love

The breeze in his bosom carried many a tale,
To be murmured to his love -
The leaf who shone like an emerald,
In the moonlight streams and sun's peeping rays.
As he stole past the isles that stretched,
Never did he stumble on treasured relics.
Nor was the she lulled by courting dew drops,
Nor was she swayed by trespassing winds.
Theirs was a love lore,
Of the leaf and the breeze.
A lore deeper than her eyes.
A lore deeper than his might.
As seasons passed, she turned pale.
So did her eyes,
As she beheld her love.
Fear struck her desires of being embraced.
As twilight turned red that day,
Reeking of decaying flesh-
Never did he sway or stumble
As he embraced her tired shivering frame.
That day he promised her a gift
Sweeter than their love,

And set on a cruise
In search of a poem.
That day, moon hid in ragged weeping clouds.
That day as he brought her
The unsung lyrics of a long-lost verse,
Gone were her moonlit eyes.
Gone was she from the branches that longed.
She was cold and shattered,
Alone with eyes that searched.
All but dirt covered her shredded face
That once cherished his lingering kiss.
Lost was she as her gift lay there,
A lost poem of souls left bare.
Lost was he and lifeless that day,
As he held a weak cold frame.
Lost was he in that nocturnal plight,
As the lost relics of his gift for her.
Never did he sore again,
Never did he wander.
Never did he fill his bosom with lore,
Of valleys that sang love songs.
As he lay still where she loved,
Lost were the lyrics and the lurking lore,
Lost was the poem of unsung souls,
Lost were the murmurs and stories.
Theirs was a love lore,
Of a leaf and the breeze.

Of unfinished dreams
And an unfinished poem.

11. You and I

"You and I", to me were not mere words,
But a whole sentence that made sense.
A whole story that breathed love.
A musing that was my flesh and blood.
"You and I", to me was a synonym-
One that meant my life and beyond.
But to you,
"You and I" was just a phrase,
A phrase that formed a part
A part so insignificant, a shredded tale
In the story solely yours.
"You and I", to you was a closed chapter,
An unfinished book.
A broken glass trodden,
Shattered beyond repair and remorse.
Here,
Here for me "and" that came between,
Was a bond to you, a bridge.
A bridge unbreakable, thought I.
Here for me it told stories of "You and I".
Here for me it was a band I tied,
A string I cherished,
A string for which I pierced my soul and flesh,

Just for me to stay connected to you.
But,
"and" was a mere 'conjunction',
A loose thread that you did tie
Around your fingertips.
So loose, to be left behind
As those fingers wriggled behind desires:
Desires that sought other 'Nouns'.
May be,
That is why "You and I" to you were mere words.
Words that never went beyond meanings;
Meanings scribbled in a lifeless dictionary.
That is why "You and I" to you,
Was possessiveness - a word you chose for my love;
The love that meant my life and beyond.
A synonym of burden was it for you,
Just as "I" turned to "burden"
And eventually into "memory".

12. Eyes that Spoke

They say that those eyes you have,
Never lie.
They say that those eyes
Are the mirror of the soul.
It reflects you and you entirely -
They say.
Then why do those fake smiles turn
A reality to you?
Then why do my pain and suffering
Still remain a tale?
Told and forgotten.
Then why does my broken soul
Remain oblivious to you?
May be...
May be my eyes no longer reflect as theirs do.
May be...
May be as my soul broke,
My eyes are broken too -
A broken shattered mirror
That never reflects
That never reveals.
Now,
I yearn for this to be true.

I yearn for my eyes to be broken,
For the truth of your ignorance
Will shatter me more.
Today I yearn for mute eyes.

13. A Shattered Soul

The lightning scared her,
The sparks blinded,
And the sounds shook her.
Yet no one listened,
No one held.
Her fears were but a tale.
Her heart sank,
She spiraled down.
Then darkness grew,
Dreams grew older -
Greyed...withered...decayed.
Her bones eroded.
Sinews loosened.
She was but a frame,
One flimsy to muse on,
And easily buried -
Treaded by onlookers and passers-by.

14. A Broken Heart ?

She wrote about broken soul,
Lost love and torn heart.
All lines similar.
All lines yearned for love and care.
Did she want to be loved?
They asked,
"Did you breakup with someone?"
A lover was what she sought and missed -
they thought.
Irony laughed along with the walls of her room.
Between the lines,
She wanted to be left behind.
To be forgotten.
To be lost.
Alone.
She wanted to never feel again,
Any feelings -
Even to feel loved,
Even happiness.

15. The Memory Lane

• 23 •

The archaic lanes
Mellow spring sang echoes now,
Festered rhapsody.

16. Love that Destroyed

He was in ruins,
A sandcastle wrecked by the waves.
The waves defended:
"It was our embrace and not fury that destroyed".
He was lost,
A leaf withered from branches in the wind.
The wind defended:
"It was my desire to carry the leaf in my arms."
He was decaying,
A rose petal withered, fading, melting into the soil.
The soil defended:
"It was my love to be with the rose."
It was love that swept him, withered him and melted him.
It was love where he lost his existence.
It was love where he longed to be destroyed,
While he became a part of her and her whole.
It was love where he became a madman,
A lunatic -
Ridiculed and shattered.
Yet in his world she was his,
And he was Hers.

17. A suicide note for you

Of all the lines I wrote
These were the most reluctant to leave.
Perhaps they knew
Once they bled into these pages,
Never will the wounds heal
And blood will freeze along the veins;
Never to brace a feeling again
Never to see you again.
Yours was a smile I adored.
A voice cherished -
A constellation of stars
Where I was never afraid to drown.
Silly it might sound
To adore eyes that never met yours.
An ode you might never see,
I wrote in papers-
Crumpled and soaked away.
As the last yellow light flickers,
This is a battle I have lost.
I know that I am loved;
But here is a heart that is too broken to hold.
Never blame or bash yourself,
For you were the one that held my string.

But here now the puppet falls
As the wind snaps the festered cords.
Escapism it is! They say...
But was I always dead or a living corpse?
A ghost with no soul,
Stranded in a crowd of blurred incantations.
Know that I loved you,
As each cup splattered coffee stains on the counter.
I loved you
As each book read and unread entered book shelf.
I loved you
As each dusk witnessed my retreating footsteps.
I loved you
As each movie night ends with you falling on me.
I loved you
As the curtains held the sunlight falling onto your eyes.
I loved you and always will
Even with me not by your side.
(Yet in those last words I never told her
All this while
She was my dream.
And the future I crafted,
Held a beautiful house;
Where we held our hands so tight
Even as wrinkles drew a painting along veins
And hair grew silver like the willow trees in wind,
Even as we drew our last breath

And held your hand so close to my heart.
But now as I leave this dream unfinished,
Let this be a chapter of my book
I hid from your sight.
Locked away with me.)

18. Old Notebook

Flipping through old notebook,
I realized the last pages held
Lonely words and letters;
Musings of a stranded mind.
As I read, I realized,
Those were treasured love letters.
Words that were never destined
To meet their destination.
Words that carried meanings,
Feelings never to be realized.
Words that muttered "I Love You"
Without spelling it out.
Words that were You and Me.
Where our names never appeared.
Those pages were our dates,
That we never went to.
Flowers we never exchanged.
Coffees we never drank.
Films we never watched.
Streets we never walked.
It was a sunset,
We never witnessed.

19. Expectations

Her soul screamed out loud,
But never did a syllable reach out to be heard.
Her fingers wriggled to express her thoughts,
But never did the ink spill out to be seen.
Her heart rose to hold destiny,
But she found herself tied up.
Tied up by strings of expectations –
'Expectations' she never possessed.

20. A Black Painting

The night seeped in dripping and crawling,
Black blood through cracked walls,
Slowly into the slimy void
That housed a queer art.
A painting he created,
A canvas torn apart –
Turned inside out
Caverning like his chest cavity.
A heart turned grey,
"Valley of Ashes" spilling dreams.
Arteries and veins tangled into oblivion,
Seeking an obtuse sort.
Lungs choked with banned desires,
Drained off air – his breath.
Does he breathe?
Does he feel?
Does he bleed?
Turned pale,
He now turns grey -
Then black.
Slowly turning into the room he is enclosed in.
The painting steadily drips to floors,
Swelling up cracks and bracing walls.

Slowly turning walls into black,
Tables, Chairs, Bed, Doors - shades of black.
Slimy black blood sealing away light,
A whole canvas with black strokes –
Roots, Veins, Nerves, Flesh, Blood.
Sealing away hope.
All seemed a deep cavern, a void -
Then the void was him.

21. Lust Transcended

When did this agonizing fervor
Steel into my poetic voice?
Was it when his roots
Entwined with my veins,
Flowering gulmohar in barren voids?
Was it when he burned into my skin
As I lay drunken from his lips?
Or was it when my life became a mime,
And me a stranded soul,
With schizophrenic dreams
Silently crawling into my bed?
They labelled me a hedonist.
But I was Aphrodite.
Mythical yet real…A tangible forgotten line,
Who craved the paradoxical love.
I starved night and day,
Hunger for love nibbling in layers.
Bruising lust left me morsels
To feel hunger caverning deep.
Feral were my dreams,
And me a cannibal, an appetite
To carve into flesh, devour him whole
Searching an ire of life.

A skeleton bereft of blood and flesh
I lay as his thoughts
Extruded into my frame
With his every breath.
I was the storm and He
The sea,
Waves slashing against each other.
Adrenaline crawling painfully…A war cry –
Each mute moan echoing a woman -
Long lost and feigned existence.
When did this agonizing fervor
Steel into my poetic voice?
Was it when my poetry
Sought transcendence?
Was it when turbulent flames
Sought kindling tames?
Now an enticing dream,
An amorous tale;
A poetic voice with
Aphrodisiac scent of life.